EXPANDED PARABLES
for
Dramatization in the Church

Robert A. Lehmann

EXPANDED PARABLES

Copyright © 1977 by
The C.S.S. Publishing Company, Inc.
Lima, Ohio

All rights reserved. No portion of this book may be reproduced or utilized in any form or by any means, electronic or mechanical including photocopying, without permission in writing from the publisher. Inquiries should be addressed to: The C.S.S. Publishing Company, Inc., 628 South Main Street, Lima, Ohio 45804.

In order to produce C.S.S. dramas, you must purchase copies sufficient for production. No additional royalty or performing fee is required.

ISBN 0-89536-062-4 PRINTED IN U.S.A.

*Dedicated to my students
in Readers Theatre
who make the relevant Scriptures
relevant*

TABLE OF CONTENTS

Preface 7

The Sower 9
           Matthew 13:1-23

The Good Samaritan 15
           Luke 10:25-37

The Unjust Steward 24
           Luke 16:1-13

The Wedding Feast 31
           Matthew 22:1-14

The Unforgiving Servant 38
           Matthew 18:21-35

The Prodigal Son 43
           Luke 15:11-32

The Rich Man and Lazarus 49
           Luke 16:19-31

The Ten Virgins 55
           Matthew 25:1-13

The Talents 60
           Matthew 25:14-30

The Great Banquet Feast 65
           Luke 14:15-24

PREFACE

These ten parables are expanded for use as dramas or Readers Theatre presentations in any Christian church. They are true to the original biblical parables but are expanded and put in script form to make them more dramatically usable and more relevant to contemporary vocabulary and thought. These parables may also serve as discussion starters for Bible classes or organizational topics.

Basically the script form is adapted for Readers Theatre presentation, that is, a group of readers who communicate the material from the manuscript to an audience through the Oral Interpretation approach of vocal and physical suggestion. Staging (placement) may be used, as well as the traditional stands and/or stools, or the script may be memorized and dramatized as necessary. A Readers Theatre presentation makes it more conducive for use by youth and persons who have little experience with drama in the church. There is also no necessity to memorize lines and therefore less rehearsal time is required. The advantage of Readers Theatre is that the cast (group) can be placed or positioned in suitable groupings in almost any chancel or church setting. When the script is done Readers Theatre style, the Narrator should be detached (but still visible) from the group to suggest his omniscience in the script.

Involvement is the key to Readers Theatre and the group should, through diligent rehearsal, try to vocally and physically suggest the character they are interpreting (not acting). When they are commenting as solos on the scene, they assume the neutral character of a modern man or modern woman who is merely reacting to the parable lines as spectators or normal listeners. A well-rehearsed and well-character-ized script should make for a meaningful, coherent message.

If more information is desired about the use of Readers Theatre in the church, *Readers Theatre Comes to the Church* (John Knox Press) by Gordon C. Bennett contains helpful suggestions.

The Sower

Matthew 13:1-23

A parable of unfruitfulness for a narrator and five solo voices (Solo 3 doubles as Isaiah and Solo 5 doubles as Jesus).

Narrator: Jesus left the house and sat by the lakeside.

Solo 1: To enjoy the peace of the waves,

Solo 2: Away from the city,

Solo 3: Away from the crowds,

Solo 4: Peace, by the waters.

Narrator: But such crowds gathered around him that he got into a boat and sat there. The people all stood on the beach, and he told them many things in parables.

Solo 4: They found him,

Solo 2: Surrounded him,

Solo 3: And begged for a story.

Solo 1: Give us a story!

Solo 4: Make us want to live!

Solo 3: Entertain us!

Narrator: So Jesus said to them:

Solo 5: Imagine a Sower going out to sow.

Solo 2: A man like me?

Solo 4: A common man?

Solo 1: A man of the soil,

Solo 3: Whose hands are rough from work?

Solo 1: Who sweats from laboring?

Solo 2: Who is bronzed by the sun,

Solo 4: Who scratches a living from the soil,

Solo 3: Who prays for rain,

Solo 2: A man like me?

Solo 5: As he sowed some seeds fell on the edge of the path, and the birds came and ate them up. Others fell on patches of rock where they found little soil and sprang up straight away, because there was no depth of soil, but as soon as the sun came up . . .

Solo 4: I thought he was a fisherman; what is all this about?

Solo 2: Shhhh!

Solo 5: But as soon as the sun came up they were scorched, and not having any roots they withered away. Others fell among thorns and the thorns grew up and choked them.

Solo 4: I like the way he tells stories. It's like they're about me.

Solo 3: I hope you're luckier than that at farming.

Solo 2: Shhhh!

Solo 5: Others fell on rich soil and produced their crop, some a hundredfold, some sixty, some thirty. Listen! Anyone who has ears.

Solo 4: Listen?

Solo 3: Listen to what? I don't get it.

Solo 1: He sure tells good stories [*Sarcastically*].

Solo 2: I'm not sure I understand.

Solo 4: I don't think you ever will; it's just a story, that's all.

Solo 3: Maybe it's a riddle.

Solo 4: He sure tells good stories. Ha!

Solo 2: I think it's too far above me.

Solo 4: It's just a story, let's go.

Narrator: Then the disciples went up to him and asked,

Solos 1-2-3-4: Why do you talk to them in riddles?

Solo 5: Because the mysteries of the kingdom of heaven are revealed to you but they are not revealed to them.

Solo 1: The mysteries of the kingdom revealed to me?

Solo 2: I don't think I understand.

Solo 5: For anyone who has, will be given more, and he will have more than enough; but from anyone who has not, even what he has will be taken away. The reason I speak to them in parables is that they look without seeing and listen without hearing or understanding. So in their case the prophecy of Isaiah is being fulfilled:

Solo 3 [Isaiah]: You will listen and listen again, but not understand; see and see again, but not perceive. For the heart of this nation has grown coarse; their ears are dull of hearing and they have shut their eyes for fear they should see with their eyes, hear with their ears, understand with their heart and be converted and be healed by me.

Solo 1: Then why do they come?

Solo 2: Why do they listen?

Solo 4: Why don't they hear?

Solo 2: Why be afraid?

Solo 1: To listen,

Solo 2: To hear,

Solo 4: To see,

Solo 1: To be converted,

Solo 1-2-4: To be healed.

Solo 5: Happy are your eyes because they see, your ears because they hear; I tell you solemnly, many prophets and holy men longed to see what you see and never saw it; to hear what you hear, and never heard it.

Solo 1: But what will it mean?

Solo 2: To have listened,

Solo 3: To have seen,

Solo 4: To be converted,

Solo 1: To be healed.

Solo 5: So you, therefore, are to hear the parable of the **sower**. When anyone hears the word of the **kingdom** without understanding, the evil one comes and carries off what was sown in his heart: This is the man who received the seed on the edge of the path.

Solo 3: It really didn't take root, Lord!

Solo 1: I just didn't understand what I was supposed to do with the seed.

Solo 4: I let it lay there hoping something would happen to it.

Solo 2: But then he came and grabbed it away.

Solo 5: The one who received it on the patches of rock is the man who hears the word and welcomes it at once with joy, but he has no root in him, he does not last; let some trial come, or some persecution on account of the word and he falls away at once.

Solo 4: I really wanted that seed to grow.

Solo 3: I watered it with joy and I listened eagerly for it to grow.

Solo 2: But then I had this problem with my neighbor —

they didn't like me always talking about this . . . this great new seed.

Solo 2: I got discouraged . . . covered it up . . . it never did grow.

Solo 5: The one who received the seed in the thorns is the man who hears the word but the worries of this world and the lure of riches choke the word and so he produces nothing.

Solo 2: I really listened, I wanted that seed to grow.

Solo 4: But I had so many other things to look after.

Solo 3: And so many places to go.

Solo 1: Got to pay for that new car; new carpet . . . takes time to work that off.

Solo 2: Put the wife to work too . . . we just didn't have time to take care of that seed.

Solo 5: And the one who received the seed in rich soil is the man who hears the word and understands it; he is the one who yields a harvest and produces now a hundredfold, now sixty, now thirty.

Solo 1: Praise God for allowing me to hear.

Solo 3: And understand.

Solo 4: For giving me the Holy Spirit who fills my heart!

Solo 2: Send me forth to sow more seed.

Solo 1: Lord, grant a bountiful harvest.

All: Amen.

The Good Samaritan

Luke 10:25-37

A parable of Christian love and concern for a narrator, Jesus, a Lawyer, and four solo voices.

Narrator: Once a Lawyer

Solo 1: a man of great position,

Solo 2: a man of respected status,

Solo 3: a man of wisdom and learning,

Solo 4: a man with great knowledge of the law,

Narrator: Once a Lawyer came and asked Jesus

Lawyer: What must I do to have eternal life?

Narrator: Jesus answered,

Solo 1: as he often did

Solo 2: with a question,

Solo 3: answered a question with a question,

Solo 4: to probe the wisdom of the questioner.

Jesus: What do the Scriptures say?

Narrator: The Lawyer answered,

Lawyer: The Scriptures say, "You must love the Lord, your God with all your soul and with all your strength and with all your mind. And it also says to love your neighbor as yourself."

Jesus: That's right. Now go and do this and you will live.

Solo 1: The Lawyer was confused by Christ's response.

Solo 2: He was not satisfied,

Solo 3: Or at least he was still anxious.

Solo 4: He still sought to catch Jesus off guard.

Lawyer: But who is my neighbor?

Solo 1: Jesus adjusted his thoughts.

Solo 2: He approached it in another way.

Solo 3: His reply would be by a familiar vehicle of his.

Solo 4: His reply would be by a parable.

Jesus: Once there was a man, a Jew, who was traveling from Jerusalem to Jericho.

Solo 2: A long way on a hot day,

Solo 4: The sun was beating down,

Solo 3: The dusty, hard ground underneath his feet,

Solo 1: No breeze to cool the sweating brow,

Solo 2: No relief for the parched lips,

Solo 3: Rocky crags surrounded the road.

Solo 1: The road was a dusty, winding road.

Solo 4: Winding all the way from Jerusalem to Jericho.

Solo 2: The rocky crags and the jagged cliffs afforded refuge for robbers,

Solo 3: [Echo] robbers . . .

Solo 4: [Echo] robbers . . .

Solo 1: Robbers, who hide in wait for lonely travelers.

Jesus: Now this man was traveling and a band of robbers fell upon him. They robbed him and beat him.

Solo 2: Nice clothes on this one.

Solo 3: And a nice bag of coins, too.

Solo 1: Let's finish him off.

Solo 4: Let him be, we have what we want.

Jesus: And they stripped him of his clothes. Then they departed and left him to die!

Narrator: And there he lay, upon that dusty, hard road, wounded, bleeding, unconscious.

Solo 1: Dying

Solo 2: [Echo] Dying . . .

Solo 3: [Echo] Dying . . .

Solo 4: [*Echo*] Dying . . .

Narrator: His only hope rested in some compassionate soul who might happen to pass by, soon . . .

Solo 1: But no one came;

Solo 2: Surely, soon, someone,

Solo 3: Someone to care.

Solo 4: And the sun beat down, the heat worsened.

Solo 3: And he lay there dying,

Solo 1: [*Echo*] dying,

Solo 2: [*Echo*] dying.

Jesus: Now, by chance, a priest was going down the road.

Solo 1: [*In a hurry moves to DC*] Oh, I'm late, I know I should never have stayed so long.

Solo 4: [*Groans as a dying man*]

Solo 1: What was that? [*Looks*] Oh, my! Someone over there . . . [*Pause*] . . . oh, what a bloody mess, the poor fellow must be dead.

Solo 2: He needs help.

Solo 3: He needs comfort and medical aid.

Solo 2: He needs a loving hand.

Solo 3: He needs a caring soul.

Jesus: When he saw him he passed by on the other side.

Solo 1: I'm so sorry about this! But I'm late for an important meeting at the synagogue [*church*]. I do hope someone comes to help him, but I just don't have the time . . . I'm late.

Narrator: And the priest hurried on, on the *other side* of the road of course.

[*Solo 1 returns to chorus position.*]

Solo 2: Muttering to himself,

Solo 3: About the importance of being on time.

Solo 2: And the sun beat down as the man lay dying.

Solo 3: [*Echo*] dying.

Narrator: A little while later another man came along the road.

[*Solo 4 walks DC and looks at the spot offstage*]

Solo 1: [*Looks*] Looks like a religious man — a Levite.
Solo 2: Yes, a man of the cloth *always* helps.

Solo 1: Surely, he will comfort him.

Solo 3: And treat his wounds and care for him.

Jesus: So, likewise, a Levite, when he came to the place and saw him, passed by on the other side.

[*Solo 4 returns to chorus position*]

Solo 2: You've got to be kidding?

Solo 3: You mean he walked right on by?

Solo 2: And the sun beating down on a dying man?

Solo 3: A man of the church walked by and ignored a dying man?

Solo 1: [*Echo*] dying,

Solo 2: [*Echo*] dying.

Narrator: Yes, more true than we care to imagine. Even those whose very profession is "loving and caring" sometimes get too involved in the pettiness of day to day existence to *care* about living.

Solo 1: But who is left to help?

Solo 3: Who really feels the hurt?

Solo 4: The agony of a tortured body?

Solo 2: The anguish of a rejected and crying person?

Jesus: But a Samaritan, as he journeyed, came to where he was.

Solo 1: [*Laughs*] This is going to be good!

Solo 4: Watch him zip by.

Solo 3: Samaritans love Jews like wounds love dirt. Ha!

Solo 2: [*Laughs*] No love lost between Jews and Samaritans.

Solo 4: The whole world knows of their ancient animosity.

Solo 3: A Samaritan wouldn't help a Jew on a bet!

Jesus: When he saw him, he had compassion.

[*Solo 2 moves to DC and looks at spot off-stage*]

Solo 1: What?

Solo 3: Really?

Solo 4: I declare!

Solo 1: You're kidding!

Narrator: Hold on there! You haven't heard the rest . . . if that shocks you, wait until you absorb what else he did.

Jesus: He went to him and bound up his wounds, pouring on oil and wine, then he set him on his own beast and brought him to an inn and took care of him.

Solo 3: This is too much!

Solo 4: Unbelievable!

Solo 1: Gave him a ride?

Solo 3: Took him to an inn?

Solo 4: You're pulling my leg!

Narrator: Would you believe there's more? Remember, love goes beyond just first-aid.

Solo 4: Take it easy, we're already bowled over!

Solo 1: We can't stand anymore shocks!

Jesus: The next day he took out a denarii ($40) and gave it to the innkeeper saying,

[*Solo 3 moves to DC position next to Solo 2*]

Solo 1 (Samaritan): Take care of him and whatever more you spend, I will repay you when I come back.

Solo 3 (Innkeeper): Is he a Samaritan like you?

Solo 2: No, he's a Jew.

Solo 3: And you're paying for his care?

Solo 2: Yes, of course.

[*Solos 2 and 3 return to chorus position*]

Narrator: See what I mean? After telling this parable, Jesus turned to the Lawyer and asked,

Jesus: Which of these three do you think proved neighbor to the man who fell among robbers?

Lawyer: [*With humility*] The one who showed mercy on him.

Solo 1: The Samaritan!

Solo 2: The one who went out of his way to comfort.

Solo 3: The one who cared.

Solo 4: The one filled with mercy.

Solo 3: The one who showed compassion.

Solo 1: The one who loved to help.

Solo 2: The one who went beyond just caring.

Solo 4: The one who truly knew the meaning of neighbor.

Narrator: And the meaning of Love.

Jesus: [*Directly to audience*] Go and do likewise!

The Unjust Steward

Luke 16:1-13

A parable of honesty and love for God, for a narrator, a rich man, an accountant, and three solo voices. The narrator doubles as Jesus.

Narrator: Now Jesus told this story,

Solo 1: To his disciples.

Solo 2: To *his* disciples.

Solo 3: To his *disciples.*

Jesus: Once there was a man,

Solo 1: A very rich man,

Solo 3: A wise man,

Solo 2: A man of position.

Jesus: He hired an accountant to handle the books.

Solo 3: The accountant was an average man.

Solo 1: He was like you.

Solo 2: He was like me.

Rich Man: Come in, sit down.

Accountant: I am . . .

Rich Man: Yes, I know, you are the applicant . . .

Accountant: Yes . . .

Rich Man: I see from your papers that you are well qualified for this job.

Accountant: I always liked working with numbers.

Rich Man: How are you at keeping books?

Accountant: Good.

Rich Man: That's fine, you're hired. You'll start tomorrow.

Accountant: Thank you, sir.

Rich Man: Of course.

Narrator: So the man was hired and he did a good job for his employer.

Solo 1: But then . . .

Solo 2: Something terrible happened,

Solo 3: A rumor went around the plant.

Narrator: The story was that the accountant was very dishonest, so . . .

Solo 3: The rich man,

Solo 1: The employer,

Solo 2: The accountant's boss,

Narrator: The Rich Man called him into his office.

Rich Man: [Moves D with accountant] What's this I hear about you stealing from me? Get your records. Get them in order. I'm going to dismiss you.

Narrator: With this, the accountant went off by himself and thought,

Accountant: I'm through! [Moves aside to think] I haven't got the strength to dig ditches and I'm too proud to beg.

Solo 2: It's too late.

Solo 1: It's all over.

Solo 3: All over!

Accountant: I have it! I have a plan and with this plan I'll have plenty of riches to take care of me when I leave.

Narrator: The accountant made appointments for all of the clients who owed his boss money . . . and the next morning, the accountant went to the office.

[Accountant moves DC]

Solo 1: The first client was there,

Solo 2: At the door,

Solo 3: Waiting to talk to the accountant.

[Solo 1 moves to downstage position]

Accountant: How much do you owe my boss?

Solo 1: I owe 850 gallons of olive oil.

Accountant: Ah, yes, here is your contract.

Solo 1: What shall I do with it?

Accountant: Take it and . . . [*Pause*]

Solo 1: Yes, go on.

Accountant: [*With authority*] Tear it up and write another contract for half that much.

[*Solo 1 returns to group*]

Narrator: So the client tore up the contract and wrote a new one for 425 gallons of oil. That very afternoon a second client came to see the accountant.

[*Solo 2 moves downstage*]

Solo 2: You wanted to see me about the bill that I owe to your employer?

Accountant: Of course, you came promptly.

Solo 2: Well, I can't pay, I . . .

Accountant: Is this your contract?

Solo 2: Yes, but I . . .

Accountant: Take it.

Solo 2: [*Very excited*] But I can't pay! I can't pay!

Accountant: Here is a pen and paper. Write a new contract for 800 bushels.

Solo 2: [*Amazed*] But I owe a thousand bushels.

Accountant: [*With authority*] Not any more!

[*Solo 2 returns to group*]

Narrator: That evening the rich man heard of the accountant's business deals with his clients.

Rich Man: [*Moves DC*] Why are you so shrewd?

Solo 1: It was a dishonest thing to do.

Solo 3: Why did you do it?

Solo 2: Why?

Solos 1, 2, 3: Why?

Rich Man: There is so much dishonesty,

Solo 3: dishonesty . . .

Solo 1: dishonesty . . .

Solo 2: dishonesty . . .

Rich Man: There is *much* more dishonesty in this world than truth.

Solo 2: truth . . .

Solo 3: truth . . .

Solo 1: truth . . .

Rich Man: But will you get to heaven by dishonesty?

Accountant: But . . .

Solo 1: No!

Accountant: I . . .

Solo 2: No!

Accountant: I . . .

Solo 3: No!

[Solos 1, 2, 3 start softly to chant "honest" when Rich Man says "honest" in the following line . . . the chant continues to the end of the line]

Rich Man: Unless you are honest in small matters, you won't be honest in large matters either.

[Solos 1, 2, 3 start softly to chant "cheat" when Rich Man says "cheat" in the following line . . . the chant continues to the end of the line]

Rich Man: Even if you cheat just a little, you won't be honest with greater responsibilities. And if you are untrustworthy . . .

Solo 2: untrustworthy . . .

Solo 1: untrustworthy . . .

Solo 3: untrustworthy . . .

Rich Man: And if you are untrustworthy about . . .

Solo 1: Anything . . .

Solo 2: Everything . . .

Solo 3: All . . .

Rich Man: Who will trust you with the riches of heaven?

Solo 1: Who?

Solo 3: Who?

Solo 2: Who?

Rich Man: If you have not been faithful in that which is another's, who will give you that which is your own?

Solo 1: No one!

Solo 2: Who can trust you?

Solo 3: Especially with the riches of heaven?

Rich Man: Neither you nor anyone else can serve two masters . . .

Solo 3: Money

Solo 2: God

Solo 1: Money

Solo 2: God

Solo 1: You shall either hate one and love the other.

Solo 3: You shall either love one and hate the other.

Solo 2: Love or hate.

Rich Man: You cannot serve both money and God.

Solo 1: You cannot buy . . .

Solo 2: Love!

Solo 3: Friendship!

Solos 1, 2, 3: God! Heaven!

The Wedding Feast

Matthew 22:1-14

A parable of the Kingdom of heaven for a narrator, a king, and three solo voices (or a narrator and four solo voices).

Narrator: And again Jesus spoke to them in parables.

Solo 1: He told them a story.

Solo 2: A story with a message.

Solo 3: A story with an inner meaning.

Narrator: And Jesus said to them: The Kingdom of heaven may be compared to a king who gave a marriage feast for his son.

Solo 1: How can the kingdom of heaven be like a marriage feast?

Solo 4: What do you suppose this guy's trying to say?

Solo 3: I've got to hear this.

Narrator: The king sent his servants to call those who were invited.

Solo 1: He had invited all the people of his kingdom.

Solo 3: The farmers,

Solo 2: The businessmen,

Solo 3: The ordinary people,

Solo 2: The important people,

Narrator: He invited them to come to the marriage feast.

Solo 4: His son was getting married.

Solo 3: He wanted them to help them celebrate.

Narrator: But they would not come; they had other things to do.

Solo 3: They made excuses.

Solo 4: I have to go work with the oxen that I just bought.

Solo 1: I just . . . got married . . . and . . . I can't come.

Solo 2: I think I have to work that afternoon. Too much work at the office.

Narrator: Everyone had something more important to do.

Solo 3: Even if it was the king's son getting married; they didn't want to take the time to go to the feast.

Solo 4: No time . . .

Solo 1: No time . . .

Solo 2: No time . . .

Narrator: And again the king sent more servants, saying,

Solo 1 (King): Tell those who are invited, Behold, I have made ready my dinner, my oxen, and my fat calves are killed, and everything is ready; come to the marriage feast.

Solo 2: He thought they didn't understand, so he asked them again,

Solo 3: To come to the wedding feast,

Solo 4: To help his son celebrate his marriage.

Solo 1 (King): Everything is ready.

Solo 3: The food,

Solo 2: The drink,

Solo 4: The music,

Solo 1 (King): It will be a wonderful feast.

Narrator: But the people he invited made light of it and went off.

Solo 3: They still weren't interested.

Solo 4: They were still too busy.

Solo 2: Too busy . . .

Solo 2, 3: Too busy . . .

Solos 2, 3, 4: Too busy . . .

Solo 3: One went off to his farm,

Solo 2: One went off to his new wife,

Solo 4: Another went to his business.

Narrator: Some became angry and seized his servants,

Solo 3: They treated them shamefully,

Solo 4: And killed them.

Solo 3: What an answer to an invitation!

Solo 4: They completely rejected the king's invitation.

Solo 2: It wasn't too much to ask of them.

Solo 4: And they didn't even feel sorry.

Narrator: The king was angry,

Solo 1: He sent his troops and destroyed those murderers,

Solo 2: and burned their city.

Solo 3: He punished the people who couldn't take the time to come to the feast.

Solo 4: He denied them the privilege to come to his feast ever again.

Narrator: Then the king said to his servants:

Solo 1 (King): The wedding is ready, but those invited were not worthy. Go therefore to the thoroughfares and invite to the marriage feast as many as you can find.

Solo 4: He was still going to celebrate,

Solo 2: but he was going to invite other people.

Solo 3: People he didn't even know.

Solo 4: People off the streets,

Solo 2: People who were strangers.

Narrator: And the servants went out into the streets and gathered all that they could find.

Solo 3: the travelers,

Solo 2: the shoppers,

Solo 4: the foreigners,

Solo 2: the good,

Solo 3: the bad,

Solo 4: so the wedding hall was filled with guests.

Narrator: But when the king came in to look at the guests, he saw there was a man who had no wedding garment; and he said to him,

Solo 1: (King): Friend, how did you get in here without a wedding garment?

Solo 3: You can't come to a wedding with dirty clothes.

Solo 2: That's insulting.

Solo 4: You have to be properly dressed.

Solo 2: You have to be acceptable to the host.

Narrator: And the man was speechless.

Solo 2: He knew he wasn't dressed properly.

Solo 4: He wasn't worthy to be at the wedding.

Narrator: And the king said to the attendants,

Solo 1 (King): Bind him hand and foot, and cast him into the outer darkness; there men will weep and gnash their teeth.

Solo 3: The king sent him away.

Solo 2: He sent him to be punished.

Solo 4: Like the people of the kingdom, this man wasn't worthy to come to the feast.

Solo 2: He wasn't acceptable to the host.

Solo 3: The king invited many people to his feast,

Solo 4: But the people of the kingdom were too busy.

Solo 2: They didn't have time.

Solo 4: They didn't think it important to come to the wedding.

Narrator: Jesus invites many people to his feast in the kingdom of heaven.

Solo 1: These people also give excuses.

Solo 4: I'm too busy.

Solo 2: I have no time.

Solo 3: I have to work that day.

Solo 4: I have other things to do.

Solo 1: And even after people do get to the feast,

Solo 2: Some aren't worthy to be there,

Solo 4: Some aren't acceptable to the host.

Solo 3: They aren't acceptable to God.

Narrator: For many are called, but few are chosen.

The Unforgiving Servant

Matthew 18:21-35

A parable of forgiveness for a Narrator, Jesus, and four solo voices who double as Peter, the Lord, Servant 1, and Servant 2.

Narrator: Many times we forget how terrific God is to us. We go around accepting what he gives us without giving anything in return to him, or if we remember him, we forget to give to people around us. Christ was speaking with his disciples one day when Peter asked him:

Solo 4 (Peter): Lord, how often shall my brother sin against me and I forgive him? As many as seven times?

Solo 1: Seven seems reasonable.

Solo 2: That's enough for anyone.

Solo 3: That's all we can expect.

Narrator: Jesus answered him;

Jesus: I tell you, not just seven times but seventy-seven times.

Solo 2: Seventy-seven times!

Solo 1: That's an awful lot.

Solo 3: Why so much?

Narrator: And Jesus told this parable to explain it.

Jesus: The Kingdom of heaven may be compared to a king who wished to settle accounts with his servants. When he began the reckoning, a man was brought to him who owed 10,000 talents ($10,000,000) and he could not pay the debt, so his Lord ordered him:

Solo 3 (Lord): You and your wife and your children and all that you own will be sold and from this, payment will be made to me.

Solo 4: He's losing everything.

Solo 2: Losing all.

Solo 4: I'm glad it's him and not me.

Solo 2: But all that money.

Solo 4: No hope of repaying that.

Solo 2: That's unbelievable.

Narrator: But the servant fell on his knees imploring him:

Solo 1 (Servant 1): Please, have patience with me and I will eventually pay you everything I owe.

Solo 2: You'll never do it.

Solo 4: Not that much.

Solo 2: Better give up — it's hopeless.

Solo 3 (Lord): I have pity for you, my servant; I am going to release you and forgive you the debt.

Solo 1: All of it?

Solo 2: All of it?

Solo 4: 10,000 talents ($10,000,000) . . .

Solo 2: Wiped out . . . just like that! [*Snaps fingers*]

Solo 3 (Lord): All . . . forgiven!

Narrator: But that same servant, as he went down the road, relieved of his burden, came upon one of his fellow servants who owed him 100 denarii ($2,000); he seized him by the throat and ordered:

Solo 1 (Servant 1): Pay the 100 denarii ($2,000) you owe to me.

Narrator: His fellow servant fell down and begged him:

Solo 2 (Servant 2): Please have patience with me, and I will eventually pay you everything I owe.

Solo 1 (Servant 1): No, if you can't pay the money, I will put you in prison till you can. That money is mine and you will repay me.

Solo 3: That scoundrel!

Solo 4: What's 10,000 talents ($10,000,000) compared to 100 denarii ($2,000)?

Solo 3: Of all the nerve.

Solo 4: He forgot, maybe?

Solo 3: How could he?

Solo 4: What a schnook!

Narrator: When the other servants saw all that had happened, they were greatly distressed and they went and reported to their lord all that had taken place.

Solo 4: He deserves to be punished!

Solo 3: Now he'll get it.

Solo 4: I knew he would!

Solo 1: Forgiven so much.

Solo 2: But not willing to forgive.

Solo 3: Hard to believe.

Narrator: Then the Lord called the servant to him and said:

Solo 3 (Lord): You wicked servant! I forgave you all of the large debt you owed because you begged and pleaded with me, but yet now you wouldn't have mercy on your fellow servant, for a smaller debt, as I did on you? For this I will have you put in jail, as I was going to do, and keep you there till you can pay all of the debt.

Solo 2: He'll be there his whole life!

Solo 4: He didn't learn.

Solo 2: No mercy.

Solo 3: Forgiveness is caring.

Solo 4: Forgiveness is mercy.

Solo 2: Forgiveness is constant.

Narrator: And having finished the parable, Christ said to Peter:

Jesus: So also my heavenly Father will do to you, if you do not forgive your brother from your heart.

The Prodigal Son
or
The Merciful Father

Luke 15:11-32

A parable of mercy and forgiveness for a Narrator, Jesus, the youngest son, the Father, and four solo voices. Solo 2 doubles as the older son.

Narrator: Dishonest tax collectors and other notorious sinners often came to listen to Jesus.

Solo 1: Because Jesus was their friend?

Solo 2: Well, they didn't have many friends; especially like Jesus.

Narrator: They came, and the Pharisees and Scribes murmured,

Solo 3: Because Jesus was an important man.

Solo 4: And important men had nothing to do with sinners!

Narrator: So Jesus told a parable.

Jesus: There was a man who had two sons; the younger of them said to his father,

Son 1: Father, give me the share of property that falls to me.

Solo 4: The son was tired of working at home.

Solo 2: He wanted to get out in the world.

Solo 1: He wanted to be on his own.

Solo 3: To be his own boss.

Jesus: So the father divided his living between them.

Solo 1: The father was sorry to see his youngest son go.

Solo 3: He knew he might never see him again.

Solo 2: It isn't easy to lose your youngest.

Solo 4: But he let him go anyway.

[*The son moves away from the group and faces upstage*]

Jesus: Not many days later, the younger son gathered all he had and took his journey to a far country where he squandered his property in loose living.

Narrator: Now, it didn't take long before this son had spent everything he had.

Jesus: And there arose a great famine in that land, and he began to be in want.

Solo 1: The crops failed that year.

Solo 2: So there was no food.

Solo 4: And money was tight.

Solo 3: Jobs were scarce.

Jesus: Being in want, the son joined himself to one of the citizens of that country who sent him into his fields to feed swine.

Solo 2: The dirtiest job around.

Solo 4: Disgusting work for a rich man's son!

Solo 3: Stinky swine.

Jesus: And he would have gladly fed on the pods that the swine ate but no one gave him anything.

Solo 1: What hunger!

Solo 4: Nothing is more anguishing.

Jesus: But when he came to himself he said,

[*Son turns to face the audience and moves slowly downstage*]

Son 1: How many of my father's hired servants have bread enough to eat and to spare, but I perish here with hunger.

Solo 2: He began to regret what he had done.

Solo 3: His hindsight was better than his foresight.

Solo 1: His former life with his father looked very good now.

Son 1: I will arise and go to my father, and I will say to him, 'Father, I have sinned against heaven and before you; I am no longer worthy to be called your son; treat me as one of your hired servants.'

Solo 2: He was willing to work for his father now.

Solo 3: But with a drastic cut in status.

Solo 4: From heir, to servant, slave . . . ironic!

Narrator: And he arose and came to his father.

[*Son moves to downstage center*]

Jesus: But while he was yet at a distance, his father saw him and had compassion, and ran and embraced him and kissed him.

[*Father moves downstage*]

Solo 4: He couldn't run very fast.

Solo 2: But he was happy to see his son back.

Solo 3: And still alive after being gone so long.

Narrator: And the son said to his father,

Son 1: Father, I have sinned against heaven and before you; I am no longer worthy to be called your son, treat me as your hired servant.

Narrator: But the father called a servant and said,

Father: Bring quickly the best robe, and put it on him; and put a ring on his hand, and shoes on his feet; and bring the fatted calf and kill it; for this my son was dead, and is alive; he was lost and is found.

Solo 1: The father was accepting him back as a full son.

Solo 4: With a robe,

Solo 3: And a ring,

Solo 1: And a celebration!

[Father and son rejoin group]

Narrator: And they began to make merry.

[Son 2 moves away]

Jesus: Now his older son was in the field.

Solo 4: He had done a long hard day of work.

Solo 3: The sun was hot.

Solo 1: He was very tired.

Jesus: And as he came and drew near to the house, he heard music and dancing. And he called one of the servants and asked what it meant.

Narrator: And he said to him,

Solo 3 (Servant): Your brother has come, and your father has killed the fatted calf, because he has received him safe and sound.

Narrator: But the elder son was angry and refused to go in.

Solo 4: He was jealous.

Solo 3: His brother was getting the royal treatment.

Solo 4: And after he wasted all his money.

Solo 1: And disappointed his father by leaving home.

[Father moves from group]

Jesus: His father came out and entreated him, but he answered his father,

Solo 2 (Son 2): Lo, these many years I have served you, and I never disobeyed your command; yet you never gave me a fatted calf that I might make merry with my friends. But when this son of yours . . .

Solo 3: He didn't want to call him brother.

Solo 4: He didn't want him back.

Solo 2 (Son 2): But when this son of yours came, who has devoured your living, you kill the fatted calf for him!

Solo 3: The wasted money was bad enough,

Solo 4: But the "welcome home" celebration was too much!

Jesus: And the father said to his older son,

Father: Son, you are always with me, and all that is mine is yours, it was fitting to make merry and be glad, for this your brother was dead, and is alive; he was lost and is found!

Narrator: Now Jesus ends the parable here and we never find out if the two brothers are reconciled or not, but the analogy is clear . .

Solo 4: God keeps accepting us time and time again,

Solo 3: When we are dead in our sins,

Solo 2: When we are lost in our selves.

Solo 1: He is truly our Merciful Father.

The Rich Man and Lazarus

Luke 16:19-31

A parable of final separation for Jesus and four solo voices. Solo 4 doubles as the Narrator, Solo 3 doubles as Abraham, and Solo 1 doubles as the Rich Man.

Narrator (Solo 4): Jesus, in talking to his disciples, told them an interesting incident, he said,

Jesus: There was a certain rich man,

Solo 1: A very rich man,

Solo 2: A man of great possessions,

Solo 3: And possessions mean power.

Jesus: There was a certain rich man who was splendidly clothed and lived each day in mirth and luxury.

Solo 4: Imagine the regal robes,

Solo 3: Plenty of entertainment every day,

Solo 1: And anything he wanted — to eat, to see, to hear.

Solo 2: What a way to live!

Jesus: One day Lazarus, a diseased beggar, was laid at his door.

Solo 2: Poor Lazarus, full of sores,

Solo 3: Tattered clothes,

Solo 4: Dirty, no doubt,

Solo 1: Begging for anything — clothes, drink, food.

Jesus: As he lay there longing for scraps from the rich man's table, the dogs would come and lick his open sores,

Solo 3: Grotesque,

Solo 1: How awful,

Solo 4: But antiseptic nevertheless.

Solo 2: The one real comfort he had, the dogs trying to heal his sores.

Solo 1: At least someone cared.

Jesus: Finally the beggar died and was carried by the angels to be with Abraham in the place of the righteous dead.

Solo 2: Poor Lazarus!

Solo 3: Perhaps he was better off.

Solo 1: It's a cinch no one really cared here on earth.

Solo 4: It was better for him in heaven.

Jesus: The rich man also died and was buried and his soul went into hell.

Solo 3: I believe it.

Solo 4: All that rich food and drink,

Solo 2: And high living.

Solo 3: He certainly deserved his fate;

Solo 4: A place in hell.

Jesus: There, in torment, he saw Lazarus in the far distance with Abraham.

Solo 4: Aha, he finally noticed Lazarus.

Solo 3: Too late now, friend.

Solo 4: What a picture — Lazarus and Abraham.

Solo 2: The poor little rich man.

Jesus: He shouted,

Rich Man (Solo 1): Father Abraham, have some pity! Send Lazarus over here if only to dip the tip of his finger in water and cool my tongue, for I am in anguish in these flames.

Solo 2: Silly fool, you want pity now.

Solo 4: You wouldn't even look at Lazarus on earth.

Solo 2: You wouldn't even give him a drink of water.

Solo 4: And now you want a drop.

Jesus: But Abraham said to him,

Abraham (Solo 3): Son, remember that during your lifetime you had everything you wanted and Lazarus had nothing.

Solo 2: That's right, you had it all.

Solo 4: And Lazarus had not a single thing.

Abraham (Solo 3): So now he is being comforted and you are in anguish.

Solo 2: God's justice?

Solo 4: Heaven and hell!

Abraham (Solo 3): Besides, there is a great chasm separating us, and anyone wanting to come to you from here is stopped at its edge; and no one over there can cross to us.

Solo 2: The distance between heaven and hell is too far to bridge.

Solo 4: Once you're in hell — you cannot go to heaven.

Solos 2, 4: You're lost!

All: FOREVER!

Jesus: Then the rich man said,

Rich Man (Solo 1): O Father Abraham, then please send him to my father's home — for I have five brothers — to warn them about this place of torment lest they come here when they die.

Solo 2: How about that, Abraham?

Solo 4: Now he wants to help his relatives.

Solo 2: After the fact!

Jesus: But Abraham said,

Abraham (Solo 3): The Scriptures have warned them again and again. Your brothers can read them anytime they want to.

Solo 2: The Bible is open to all the living.

Solo 4: All they have to do is open it — and read — and believe the Good News.

Jsus: But the rich man replied,

Rich Man (Solo 1): No Father Abraham, they won't bother to read them.

Solo 2: Too busy no doubt!

Solo 4: Too many other important business matters to attend to!

Rich Man (Solo 1): But if someone is sent to them from the dead, then they will turn from their sins.

Solo 2: Oh, some kind of magic show you want?

Solo 4: Raising from the dead?

Solo 2: And just like that they'll shake and tremble in fear and fall on their knees and beg forgiveness.

Solos 2, 4: And pray.

Jesus: But Abraham said:

Abraham (Solo 3): If they won't listen to Moses and the prophets, they won't listen even though some rises from the dead.

[*Solos 1, 2, 3, 4 move as a group to DC*]

Solo 2: Each man is responsible for his own life.

Solo 4: No one else can believe for him.

Solo 1: When men die, their fates are fixed.

Solo 3: When they are living — then they must accept Christ.

Narrator (Solo 4): [*Moves away to a Narrator position*] But for many people it's a case of, "*Now* they will not, *then* they cannot."

Solo 2: We leave it there.

Solo 1: We can only state our own faith.

Solo 3: The cross must have meaning for all men,

Solos 1, 2, 3: Wherever they may be.

The Ten Virgins

Matthew 25:1-13

A parable of the Kingdom of heaven for a narrator, Jesus, and four solo voices.

Narrator: There are always people who are unprepared; not ready for work, for meals, for events — they just seem to "put things off" naturally. That may be acceptable when dealing with earthly matters but when it concerns heavenly matters, it is tragic. Jesus said:

Jesus: The Kingdom of heaven can be illustrated by the story of ten bridesmaids who took their lamps to meet the bridegroom.

Solo 1: Sounds like a big wedding!

Solo 2: Ten bridesmaids,

Solo 3: Waiting for the great event,

Solo 4: Going out to meet the bridegroom.

Solo 3: What joy!

Solo 2: What anticipation!

Jesus: But only five of them were wise enough to fill their lamps.

Solo 4: Only half really prepared?

Solo 1: Only half looked ahead?

Solo 3: Only half thought of necessities?

Solo 1: Only half?

Jesus: While the other five were foolish and forgot.

Solo 3: Foolish — you know it.

Solo 2: To forget a little thing like fuel.

Solo 1: That's not even thinking.

Solo 4: Half of them — unprepared.

Jesus: So, when the bridegroom was delayed, they lay down to rest until midnight.

Solo 2: Probably a long wait.

Solo 3: One can get awfully tired just waiting, with nothing to do.

Solo 4: Waiting gets long when you're excited.

Solo 1: Especially when waiting for a great event.

Solo 3: I do wish he'd come!

Solo 4: What's taking him so long?

Jesus: At midnight they were roused by the shout,

Solo 2: "The Bridegroom is coming! Come out and welcome him."

Solo 1: He's coming!

Solo 3: He's here!

Solo 4: Let's run to meet him.

Solo 1: Let's hurry!

Jesus: All the girls jumped up and trimmed their lamps.

Solo 3: We must be prepared.

Solo 4: Quick, fix your lamps.

Solo 1: Trim the wick.

Jesus: Then the five who hadn't any oil begged the others to share with them, for their lamps were going out.

Solo 1: Let us have some of your oil.

Solo 3: Yes, our lamps are going out.

Solo 4: We really need such a little! Just enough to last through the night.

Jesus: But the others replied.

Solo 2: We haven't enough. Go instead to the shops and buy some for yourselves.

Solo 1: Quick, let's run.

Solo 3: Yes, before the festivities begin.

Solo 4: Hurry, let's go.

Jesus: But while they were gone, the bridegroom came, and those who were ready went in with him to the marriage feast.

Solo 2: They were ready.

Solo 3: They came prepared.

Solo 1: They planned ahead.

Solo 4: They anticipated.

Jesus: Those who were ready went in with him to the marriage feast, and the door was *locked.*

Solo 1: Locked tight!

Solo 2: Sealed shut!

Solo 3: Closed!

Solo 4: Closed!

Solo 1: Closed!

Jesus: Later, when the other five returned, they stood outside calling,

Solos 1, 3, 4: Sir, open the door to us!

Solo 3: Let us come in!

Solo 4: We've come back!

Solo 1: Now we're ready!

Jesus: But he called back,

Solo 2: "Go away! It is too late!"

Solo 3: You mean we can't enter?

Solo 1: But we're ready now!

Solo 4: Please, we're sorry!

Solo 2: It is too late!

[*All three rapidly in disbelief*]

Solo 3: Too late?

Solo 1: Too late?

Solo 4: Too late?

Jesus: So stay awake and be prepared, for you do not know the day nor the hour when the Son of Man will return.

[*Solos 1, 2, 3, 4 move as a group DC*]

Solo 1: Now is the time to prepare.

Solo 3: Now is the time to be ready.

Solo 4: Now is the time!

Solo 2: [*Pause*] Now.

The Talents

Matthew 25:14-30

A parable of stewardship for a narrator and four solo voices. Solo 4 doubles as Servant 1, Solo 2 doubles as Servant 2, and Solo 1 doubles as Servant 3.

Narrator: The Kingdom of heaven can be illustrated by the story of a man going into another country, who called his servants together and loaned them money to invest for him while he was gone.

Solo 1: He called them because they belonged to him.

Solo 2: He trusted them.

Solo 3: He gave what he had to them.

Solo 4: To invest.

Solo 2: To gain more.

Solo 3: To use wisely.

Solo 1: Just as the Lord gives talents to us.

Narrator: He gave five talents ($5,000) to one, two talents ($2,000) to another, and one talent ($1,000) to the last.

Solo 4: Five talents ($5,000)!

Solo 2: Two talents ($2,000)!

Solo 1: One talent ($1,000)!

Narrator: So . . . five talents, two talents, one talent . . . (money) dividing it in proportion to their abilities . . . and then he left on his trip to another country.

Solo 3: Dividing it in proportion to their abilities?

Solo 4: [*To himself*] Hmmm, five talents ($5,000) . . . what shall I do with it?

Solo 2: [*To himself*] Well now, two talents ($2,000) . . . to invest; let's see . . .

Solo 1: [*To himself*] One talent ($1,000) is a lot of responsibility.

Narrator: The man who received the five talents ($5,000) began immediately to buy and sell with it and soon earned another five talents ($5,000).

Servant 1 (Solo 4): I knew I could invest and make it grow so that my master could gain from it.

Solo 3: He used talents (money) wisely!

Solo 1: Yes, but he had a lot more to work with . . .

Solo 3: He used his wisely!

Narrator: The man with the two talents ($2,000) went right to work too and earned another two talents ($2,000).

Servant 2 (Solo 2): That wasn't difficult . . . to double the talents . . . to serve the master.

Solo 3: He used his wisely also.

Solo 1: Just luck, that's all! He could have lost it all.

Solo 3: He used his wisely.

Narrator: But the man who received the one talent ($1,000) dug a hole in the ground and hid the money for safe keeping.

Servant 3 (Solo 1): I'm not going to lose any of this . . . I'll just tuck it away and then no one will take it and I won't lose it.

Solo 3: Not so wise!

Solo 4: Poor fellow; to hide what his master gave him to use.

Solo 3: Not so wise!

Narrator: After a long time their master returned from his trip and called them to him to account for his money.

Master (Solo 3): My men, come, I have returned . . . account for your stewardship.

Narrator: The one to whom he had entrusted the five talents ($5,000) brought him ten talents ($10,000).

Servant 1 (Solo 4): Master, here I have gained another five talents ($5,000) for you.

Master (Solo 3): You have been faithful in handling this small amount, so now I will give you many more responsibilities. Begin the joyous tasks I have assigned to you.

Narrator: Next came the man who had received the two talents ($2,000) with the report,

Servant 2 (Solo 2): Sir, you gave me two talents ($2,000) to use, and I doubled it.

Master (Solo 3): Good work, you are a good and faithful servant. You have been faithful over this small amount, so now I will give you much more.

Narrator: Then the man with the one talent ($1,000) came and said,

Servant 3 (Solo 1): Sir, I knew you were a hard man, and I was afraid you would rob me of what I earned so I hid your money in the earth and here it is!

Master (Solo 3): Wicked man! Lazy servant!

Solo 4: [Aside] Poor fellow.

Solo 2: [Aside] Poor steward.

Master (Solo 3): Since you knew I would demand your profit, you should at least have put my money into the bank so I could have some interest.

Solo 2: At least earned a small percentage.

Solo 4: At least used the talent a little.

Master (Solo 3): Take the money from this man and give it to the man with the ten talents ($10,000).

Solo 2: Yes, sir.

Servant 1 (Solo 4): To me, sir? Why?

Master (Solo 3): The man who uses well what he is given shall be given more, and he shall have abundance. But from the man who is unfaithful, even what little responsibility he has shall be taken from him.

Solo 2: The man who is a wise steward of his talents will be blessed.

Solo 4: The man who does not use those that he has or abuses them, shall wither and die.

Master (*Solo 3*): Throw the useless servant out into outer darkness.

Solo 2: Out . . . [*Move DC*]

Solo 4: Into darkness . . . [*Move beside Solo 2 DC*]

Master (*Solo 3*): There shall be weeping . . .

Solo 2: Weeping,

Master (*Solo 3*): And gnashing of teeth . . .

Solos 2, 4: Gnashing of teeth.

[*Pause*]

Solo 1: [*To audience*] I did not use the talents wisely.

Solo 2: [*To audience*] What do you do with yours?

Solo 4: [*To audience*] Do they serve your Master?

The Great Banquet Feast

Luke 14:15-24

A parable of God's Kingdom for a Narrator, the Master, and four solo voices.

Narrator: When Jesus finished telling the parable of the marriage feast, a man sitting at the table with Jesus exclaimed,

Solo 3: What a privilege it would be to get into the Kingdom of God!

Solo 1: He was fascinated by the story.

Solo 2: He was moved by the great things Jesus told.

Solo 4: How God will reward those who open their hearts to the unfortunate.

Solo 1: Jesus replied with this illustration.

Narrator: A man prepared a great feast and sent out many invitations. When all was ready, he sent his servant around to notify the guests that it was time for them to arrive.

Solo 2: [*Calling to those on the right*] Come, for all is now ready. [*Pause, calling to those on the left*] Come, for all is now ready.

Solo 1: Oh, it's time for the banquet already?

Solo 4: You're ready now?

Solo 3: Really, I didn't think you'd call so soon.

Solo 2: Come, for all is now ready!

Solo 1: I don't think I can arrange it.

Solo 3: I don't get organized that fast.

Solo 4: I've got so much to do.

Narrator: They all began making excuses.

Solo 1: I . . . er . . . ah . . . I just bought a field and I must go out and see it; I pray you, have me excused.

Solo 2: Likely story . . . you must go to inspect it today!

Solo 4: Well, it sounds logical.

Solo 3: You can't afford to neglect your business.

Narrator: Another came with this excuse:

Solo 3: I just bought five pair of oxen and need to try them out; I pray you, have me excused.

Solo 2: Likely story . . . you must go to try them today!

Solo 4: You need to make sure you get a good product.

Solo 1: That's his work . . . it's important.

Narrator: And yet another came with this excuse:

Solo 4: I . . . er . . . ah . . . um . . . I . . . ah . . . have married . . . a wife . . . and therefore I cannot come; I pray you, have me excused.

Solo 2: Likely story . . . you must be with your wife today.

Solo 1: You need to take care of your family.

Solo 4: Your home . . . it's important.

Narrator: The servant returned and reported to his master what they had said.

Solo 2: One said he bought a field and wanted to go to see it. Another said he bought some oxen and wanted to try them out. And another said he just got married and had to stay home . . . they all asked to be excused.

Narrator: Then the master was very angry and said,

Master: [*To his servant*] Go out quickly to the streets and lanes of the city, and bring the poor and crippled and blind and lame.

Solo 4: Maybe they will appreciate it and aren't so busy!

Solo 3: Maybe they will be prepared and have no excuses!

Solo 1: Maybe they will not have so many important things to do!

Narrator: And the servant did this and came and reported to his master,

Solo 2: Sir, what you commanded has been done and still there is room.

Narrator: And the Master said,

Master: [*To the servant*] Well then, go out to the highways and hedges, and compel people to come in, that my house may be filled.

Solo 4: Drag in all those beggars?

Solo 1: All those pitiful poor.

Solo 3: All those ragged wretches.

Master: Urge anyone you find to come, so my house will be full. For none of those invited first will get even the smallest taste of what I prepared for them.

Solo 2: [*To audience*] They were too occupied with the things of this worldly life.

Solos 1, 3, 4: [*To audience*] Are you?